21 DAYS FOR PEACE

ISBN: 9798987963104
Cover Design & Layout: Zainab Mustapha
Cover Photography: Kelvin Holtzclaw

Printed in the United States of America

Live Peace Live Truth

Introduction

As we enter into this journey, maybe some of us are looking to rediscover our peace and others of us may be seeking to find it for the first time. Wherever we find ourselves in this journey, just know that we are here together. I encourage you to find something that you are willing to sacrifice for these 21 days, something that distracts you or something that you know you need to give up anyway. When you think of doing that thing, let it be your reminder to come and have your devotion time with the Father.

I don't claim to be an expert in peace by any stretch of the imagination, but I have received a charge from the Father to invite you on this journey with me. As I write, I am taking this journey with you and praying for and with you. We all struggle with maintaining our peace at times, but peace is a promise of our heavenly Father. He is our Jehovah Shalom, which translates to "God of peace." As we walk with Him and follow after Him, we find Him to be our peace in every circumstance and situation. So, come and take this journey with me. I cannot promise to have all of the answers, but I can promise to point to scripture that highlights God's plan and purpose for us as it pertains to our peace and to help us to reconcile that with our daily life.

I pray peace and blessings over each of you and that by the time you have completed this journey, you feel better equipped to respond to troubles with the truth of

God and to walk in peace even when there may be chaos around you.

Day 1
Anxious for what?
Philippians 4:6-7

I begin here because this scripture has been my "stand on" scripture for quite some time. As someone who has battled anxiety for many years, this scripture is where I have found a great source of peace in my life. "Be anxious for nothing, but in everything by prayer and supplication, with thanksgiving, let your requests be made known to God; and the peace of God, which surpasses all understanding, will guard your hearts and minds through Christ Jesus."

It took me some time to grasp this because so many times I missed a key piece of these verses, "with thanksgiving." Why with thanksgiving?

Well, 1 Thessalonians 5:18 tells us to "in everything give thanks; for this is the will of God in Christ Jesus for you." I believe that is a very key reason that the thanksgiving piece is so important. This is the will of God for us "in everything."

When things are good, give thanks; when things are not so good, give thanks.

Why?

Because no matter the circumstance, God is still good. That is His nature.

So Philippians 4:6-7 tells us to be anxious for nothing, but then it gives us the instructions on what to do instead of being anxious. We are to pray and supplicate our requests to God with thanksgiving, but how do we do this?

Whatever it is that is threatening our peace, threatening to cause us stress, we pray and supplicate and present that thing to the Father who is so faithful and so able to carry it. When we supplicate we are earnestly pleading with God to take this thing from us and then we thank Him and praise Him in advance. We thank Him for peace that He is bringing, we thank Him in advance because we believe that it is already done and we thank Him for just being a God who hears and knows us. As the scripture goes on to tell us, after we have done these things, *then* the peace of God, which passes all understanding, will guard our hearts and minds through Christ Jesus. It will be a peace that we cannot explain and that many will not understand, but His peace will come in and cover us and guard our hearts and our minds. Those anxious thoughts and feelings won't be able to come in because of the peace that guards us.

I encourage you today to present those things to the Father. When you feel those anxious thoughts trying to come, surrender them. Go to God in prayer and tell Him what is troubling you. Yes, He already knows, but when we pray and surrender them, it is an act of humility, telling God that we are inviting Him to come into our situations and take control. When we surrender it, we must take our hands off of it and allow Him to move. Just begin to thank Him for working and moving on your behalf even when you can't see it yet.

Let us pray:

Father, we know that things are seeming overwhelming right now. We know that so much is on our plates and we do not know how to handle it, but we know that You are God and that You see our needs and are able to intervene on our behalf. So God, right now we ask that You come in and take control. Have Your way in our lives and take control of every situation. Father we trust You to be God in our lives and in our situations and we know that, with You, we can handle it. Father, we thank You now for working and moving. We thank You for taking away the weight of stress and anxiety and for granting us Your peace. Father, right now we pray that Your peace go with us throughout this and everyday and that You give us the grace to handle all that we face today and everyday. This is our humble prayer in the precious name of Christ Jesus, Amen.

Day 2
Discouraged or Cheerful?
John 16:33

Often times we become overwhelmed by so much and we must make a conscious decision to walk in discouragement or to be of good cheer. Today we go to John 16:33 where Jesus is talking to the disciples as He is preparing to leave them because He knows the time is coming when He will be betrayed and sacrificed.

He says to them, "These things I have spoken to you, that in Me you may have peace. In the world you will have tribulation; but be of good cheer, I have overcome the world.'"

Can any of us relate to having times of tribulation? I know I can.

I have had times that I did not know which way was up and how I would get through all that I was dealing with, but God. Jesus tells the disciples that the things that He has spoken to them, through parables and all that He has shared was so that, in Him, they may have peace.

I believe that we can take this for ourselves today as well, that we can read the teachings of Jesus and find peace therein. Jesus shares a great deal through His parables and teachings. There is so much knowledge and wisdom to be found there. He even warns the disciples that the world will hate them.

We may be wondering, so how does that bring me peace?

Well, I'm so glad you asked. Jesus shares that the world hated him first (John 15:18). If we look back to John 16:33, we find that He says He wrote these things that they might have peace in Him and then He tells them that they will have tribulation, but to be of good cheer.

How can we be of good cheer in the midst of tribulations?

I believe the key to that lies in the "in Me." Jesus is not telling them to have peace within themselves, but to have peace in Him. Just as He is telling us today to have peace in Him.

We cannot do it within ourselves. Trying to find peace in self, we will fail every time and we will find ourselves choosing discouragement over and over again, but when we seek peace in Jesus, we will surely find it every time.

Looking back to yesterday, we talked about surrendering our struggles to the Father so that He can carry them and we release that weight from ourselves. Just the same way, we seek our peace through Jesus Christ, the one who was and is and is to come.

Remember, He is Jehovah Shalom, "God of peace." He is our peace and so we will always find it in Him.

Then, we close out that verse with the instructions that sound so simple, "be of good cheer, I have overcome the world."

Y'all this is it right here. This is why we can find our peace in Him, because He has already overcome it. Every problem, every trial, every tribulation, every struggle, every issue, even those that we never even talk about, He has overcome them all. There is not a place we go that He has not already been. There is nothing we go through that He has not already overcome and guess what? He is fighting for US! The One who has already overcome the world, the One who has conquered death, hell and the grave, He is fighting for us. That is why we can be of good cheer. That is why we can find our peace in Him. He has already conquered everything that attempts to threaten our peace.

Let us pray:
Father today, I am grateful for Your peace. I am grateful for Your loving kindness, Your grace and Your mercy toward me. Father I thank You for being my peace. Thank You for being the one that I can trust and hope in and find confidence in. Father, thank You for being my mighty conqueror. Thank You for overcoming the world. Today, I pray and ask that You go into every hidden area, every place that I am thinking that I cannot possibly surrender to You and God, I surrender it. I give You control. I know that You have overcome the world and in comparison, my issue is small and minuscule and You can handle it. I know that Your plan for me is peace and I move myself out of the way that I may find my peace in You. You are trustworthy and You already have it handled. I take my hands off of it and exchange it for Your peace. I thank You and praise You in advance because I know that it is already done and Father, I choose to be of good cheer. In the precious name of Christ Jesus I pray, Amen.

Day 3
So…He's with me?
Matthew 28:19-20

Today we look at the end of the gospel according to Matthew. We see where Jesus has been resurrected and the disciples came to worship Him, but some doubted and this is the charge that He gave them. However, we see that with this charge, He reminded them that He is with them. He says, "Go therefore and make disciples of all the nations, baptizing them in the name of the Father and of the Son and of the Holy Spirit, teaching them to observe all things that I have commanded you; and lo, I am with you always, even to the end of the age." Amen."

God does not charge us to do anything alone. He is always with us.

Often times, we find ourselves distressed when trying to walk out a charge that God has given us. The problem is that we try to do it in self.

We hear God calling, we know what He has said, but we forget to follow Him. We forget that He is with us. We become overwhelmed and we get discouraged (yesterday's study) because nothing seems to be going according to plan.

So how do we deal with this?

Well, let's return to the scripture. He gives the disciples a charge to go and make disciples of all the nations. Let's be honest, that can sound like a daunting task. We're like, God you want me to do what?

I can honestly say I believe that is why He proceeds to provide that reassurance, especially if we consider that in the verses preceding, the scriptures say that some of them were doubting.

So, we're already doubting and then God provides this seemingly daunting charge, He knows us, He knows our very nature and our thoughts so He knows what is going through our heads. Instead of speaking to the unbelief, He provides reassurance. "I am with you always, even to the end of the age." That reads peace to me.

I know this sounds like a lot, I know you can't do it on your own, but I am with you. You can rest in Me, you can reside in Me, you can trust in Me, you can hold onto Me because I am with you.

Today, let us remember that as we walk through the individual charges that God has given us. It may seem like a lot, it may be out of our comfort zones and it may even seem like something that we just cannot do, but God said that He is with us. Always.

That is a recipe for peace. The simple remembering that He is with us…always.

Let us pray:
Father, today we look to You for guidance in what You have given us to do. We want to be obedient in what You have blessed our hands to do and we want to do it to the glory of You. Father, we want You to be pleased in our actions. As we journey through this day, we ask that You keep us reminded that You are with us. Let us not forget that You are always right there. Give us the

wisdom and the knowledge to carry out every assignment that You have charged us with and help us to do them well. Father, we trust You in all things and we know that You are the author and the finisher of our faith. Let us find peace in knowing that You are with us and that You have not led us to any place that You have not already been. Thank You for preparing the way before us and for the peace in knowing that the path is already set as long as we follow after You. Today, we ask that You anoint our hands to do Your work to Your glory and continue to maintain our peace on the journey. Thank You just for being with us. In the mighty and precious name of Jesus we pray, Amen.

Day 4
Why Worry?
Matthew 6:25-33

I know our text is a little lengthy today, but I promise it has purpose. As I stated at the beginning, I am journeying through this as I am writing. For this day, God gave me this reminder, and it seemed so fitting to pass on so let's look at this together.

This scripture passage is taken from Jesus's sermon on the mount and He is reminding us not to worry.

It reads, "Therefore I say to you, do not worry about your life, what you will eat or what you will drink; nor about your body, what you will put on. Is not life more than food and the body more than clothing? Look at the birds of the air, for they neither sow nor reap nor gather into barns; yet your heavenly Father feeds them. Are you not of more value than they? Which of you by worrying can add one cubit to his stature? "So why do you worry about clothing? Consider the lilies of the field, how they grow: they neither toil nor spin; and yet I say to you that even Solomon in all his glory was not arrayed like one of these. Now if God so clothes the grass of the field, which today is, and tomorrow is thrown into the oven, will He not much more clothe you, O you of little faith? "Therefore do not worry, saying, 'What shall we eat?' or 'What shall we drink?' or 'What shall we wear?' For after all these things the Gentiles seek. For your heavenly Father knows that you need all these things. But seek first the kingdom of God and His righteousness, and all these things shall

be added to you. Therefore do not worry about tomorrow, for tomorrow will worry about its own things. Sufficient for the day is its own trouble."
Sounds easy enough, right? The birds are fine, the lilies are fine, the grass is fine and we are more important than these things so if the Father takes care of them, how much more will He care for us? What do we have to worry about?

The reality is that as easy as this sounds in theory, we still worry. We say what shall we eat, what shall we drink and what shall we wear when resources are running low.

Why wouldn't we? We are human, right? It is natural for us to have concerns, especially when things are looking crazy.

I encountered a situation while writing for this day where my paycheck for the week was going to be cut short due to circumstances that I had no control over. I started to worry, but I remembered that God is a keeper and He is my provider. My job is a resource, but He is the source and He is the Well that never runs dry. So I choose to seek Him first and trust that all other things will be added. I also trust that no matter what it looks like, He will provide!

This can sound easy to encourage others in when things are going good for us and easy to talk about in theory, but when we are in it, that is where the true test of faith comes.

Even in that, He gives us instructions for how to get through, for how to maintain our peace and how to avoid worrying.

Worrying leads to stress and stress destroys our peace. So Jesus tells us, to seek first the Kingdom of God and His righteousness and then all these things that we are worrying about will be added. Sounds like Philippians 4:6-7 to me.

We put our focus on the Kingdom of God and His righteousness as opposed to worrying about our physical needs and as we focus on Him, He provides our physical needs.

When we stop worrying, we see Him working. It's like the saying "a watched pot never boils." If we are constantly looking at what is not happening, it, one, seems to take FOREVER and two, we miss so many great things that are happening around us.

If we are constantly looking at this pot waiting for it to boil, we miss interactions with our family around us, the opportunity to begin to prepare other parts of our meal or just being able to focus on something else to pass the time while waiting. It can also become stressful waiting for that pot to boil if we may be in a rush.

Just the same, if we are focused on our problems and issues waiting for them to change, we miss out on the opportunity to commune with God, to enjoy the teaching and edification that comes from spending time in His word and we neglect so much around us because we have had our focus in the wrong place. We can alleviate that stress when we put our focus on the Father. We can seek Him, commune with Him, learn from Him and trust Him to provide. When we put our focus in the right place, we don't have to worry because we trust God to remain true to His character and to meet our needs. So why should we worry when we serve an all powerful King who is able and willing to supply all of our needs if we would just trust Him. Today, let us walk in the peace of knowing that He is our Jehovah Jireh, "God who provides."

Let us pray:
Father we come before You today admitting that we have needs. We admit that we sometimes worry where our resources will come from and we worry that we may not have enough. Father, today we ask that You forgive us for failing to trust You in these areas and that You help us to re-shift our focus. Father we look to You because we know who You are and we know that You are our source. All other things are just resources. We trust You to be Jehovah Jireh, We trust You to keep us in perfect peace. Father we thank You that we can look to You and know that You are where our help comes from. Help us to keep our focus on You. Father, You have our full attention. Show us Your ways and continue to lead us and guide us into Your peace. We trust You in all things. In the name of Christ Jesus we pray, Amen.

Day 5
Think on what?
Philippians 4:8-9

Have you ever received a bad report from a doctor and did not know where to go from there? News like that can be a harsh attack on our peace. How do we avoid thinking about it all day when that is literally the only thing on our mind?

Philippians 4:8-9 gives us some alternatives to assist us in regaining our peace, "Finally, brethren, whatever things are true, whatever things are noble, whatever things are just, whatever things are pure, whatever things are lovely, whatever things are of good report, if there is any virtue and if there is anything praiseworthy —meditate on these things. The things which you learned and received and heard and saw in me, these do, and the God of peace will be with you."

This is what we can think on:

1) Those things that are true.

I heard my previous pastor say often that the doctor can give you facts, but it is God who holds the truth. That is what we choose to think on. When the news isn't good and it attempts to threaten our peace, we think on the truth that the Father brings. His truth is that by the stripes of Jesus we are healed (Isaiah 53:5). We can stand on that. We can take God at His Word and at His character. His character speaks where there may not be words.

2) Those things that are noble.

God is noble. He is honorable. He is deserving of our attention and our respect. He is the one that we can put our trust in and He is the one who makes all things good. We can lean on Him, we can believe in Him, we can take Him at His Word and when things are hard, His nobility is an excellent place to focus.

3) Those things that are just.

We think on those things that bring honor to ourselves and to others, not those things that would tear one another down. We do not tear ourselves down with negative thoughts; however, we build ourselves up with the just revelation of the Word of God.

4) Those things that are pure.

We can think on that which is pure from the Father. We avoid focusing on that which has been tainted by our fears and unwholesome talk.

5) Those things that are lovely.

These are the things that are beautiful, such as the unfailing love of the Father. He is lovely and His love is lovely. The thoughts that He has for us are lovely (Jeremiah 29:11).

6) Those things that are of good report.

Finally, we find the good things, the positive things. The things that shine positive light and tell of the goodness of the Lord. We can always find something of good report to think of because God is always good. We just sometimes must shift our focus.

This is how we get to the virtue and that which is praiseworthy. God is forever worthy of our praise, no matter what things look like.

Once we focus on these things and take our focus off of the negative things, we find ourselves walking in peace because the God of peace, Jehovah Shalom, is with us.

It can be hard to focus on these things when there is so much that seems to be wrong around us, but we must make an intentional decision to walk in peace daily. That decision includes making the effort to shift our focus from what seems to be wrong, to what we know about God and what He is doing right for us. I promise if we look for it, we will find it.

Let us pray:

Father, we just want to take a moment to thank You for being God. We thank You for Your truth that we can stand on and we thank You for Your goodness. Father, today we ask that You help us to re-shift our focus. We know that things are tough and bad news seems to be coming on every hand, but we are so grateful that You love us enough to remind us of Your goodness, even in a hard situation. Father we choose to think on that which is true, that which is honest, that which is just, that which is pure, that which is lovely and that which is of good report. We make a conscious effort to think on these things and we recognize that we need Your help to remain focused. Father please help us to stay focused and we trust and believe that as we focus on Your truth, that Your peace will follow us everywhere we go. Thank You for Your peace. We pray this in the name of Christ Jesus, Amen.

Day 6
Who's scared?
Psalms 56:3-4

If we're honest, we face things often, maybe even daily that can cause us to be afraid. For those of us who are persons of color, things became quite scary at the end of May and beginning of June of 2020. We may have found ourselves angry and each person was seeking the best response.

The reality is that each person will respond differently to their fears and it does not make any one of us better than the other. Fear is a very real emotion and it will definitely threaten our peace.

Fear brings about so many different emotions and stress can be a response to fear.

Fear of the unknown brings about stress and anxiety. When we do not know what to expect next or when we fear that our lives are in danger, peace is not necessarily our first response.

That is where David finds himself in this psalm. He had been captured and I am sure that fear was a very real emotion for him, but his response was faith in God. That was how he maintained his peace.

It reads, "Whenever I am afraid, I will trust in You. In God (I will praise His word), In God I have put my trust; I will not fear. What can flesh do to me?"

That is how we too can maintain our peace. We respond with trust in God. We recognize that yes, I am afraid. Yes, things seem uncertain right now. Yes, I do not know what to do next. Yes, I feel that whatever I do could cost me greatly, but God I will trust in You. I know that you are my protecter and my keeper. I know that You hold the world in Your hands. I know that You work everything according to the good counsel of Your will (Ephesians 1:11).

This is how we get through. This is how we continue through. Let's be honest, trouble does not come one time and end, but it happens often enough. In order to continue to get through the tough times, we must be able to choose this response over and over again. We can make this our daily declaration.

"God no matter what I face today, I will trust in You and I will not be afraid."

It is a daily decision we must make again and again. As I often heard my previous pastor state, this is not something that we graduate from. We do not graduate from christianity, but we are continually in the sanctification process and each day we are faced with choices of how we are going to respond to what we face.

Will we choose fear or will we choose faith? That is literally the difference between peace and turmoil, between peace and anxiety. I choose faith, I pray that you will do the same.

Let us pray:
Father, we admit that we are afraid. We admit that things are rough and that times are hard. Father, above all, we admit that we need You. We welcome You

23

in. We ask You to come and pour out Your peace upon us. Father, we pray that You would intervene in our situations. We invite You into them and we do not ask You to sit on the sidelines while we try to work them out on our own. Father, we trust You. We choose faith today. We choose to walk in the perfect peace that You bring as opposed to the anxiety that the enemy desires us to choose. Father, today and everyday we declare that no matter what we face, we will trust in You and we will not be afraid. We recognize that we may be making this declaration while afraid, but Father we believe that as we daily make this declaration, we will feel the grip of fear start to release us and that Your peace will bring us the comfort that we so desperately need. Father, thank You for being God, thank You for loving us, thank You for protecting us and thank You for being our peace. This and all things we ask in the precious name of Jesus Christ our Lord and our Savior, Amen.

Day 7
Humility…really?
1 Peter 5:6-7

Have you ever been overzealous?
You know, just eager to accomplish a goal or task
without fully thinking it through?
I think we can often find ourselves being overzealous
even for the things of God. There is nothing wrong
with being zealous for the things of God, it is an
important quality for His people, but when we are
overzealous, we find ourselves sometimes thinking too
highly of ourselves and operating in flesh.
Today's scripture reminds us of how we should operate
in order to maintain our peace when going after the
things of God. "Therefore humble yourselves under
the mighty hand of God, that He may exalt you in due
time, casting all your care upon Him, for He cares for
you."
Humility can seem an easy feat to some and very hard
to others. Whether easy or hard, it is vital to the life of
every believer and it is one of our keys to Godly peace.
When we humble ourselves, we remove our own
selfish ambitions and we allow God's will to prevail.
Humility involves allowing God's purposes to be
achieved in us and not seeking to advance our own
agendas.
Isn't that freeing?
Let's be real, I know it isn't always. I know it can be
hard at times, especially when we do not know what is
coming next, but the good news is that we serve a God

who is trustworthy. As we already discussed, we can trust Him at His word and at His character. We can trust that His plans for us are good, even those that are unknown, and that should bring us peace.

This scripture reminds us that we should humble ourselves before the Father and allow Him to exalt us in the proper time.

When we are overzealous and attempt to exalt ourselves, we end up with improper timing which can cause anxiety and threaten our peace.

When we put our trust in the Father and cast our cares upon Him, we can rest in the comfort and knowledge that He knows best and His timing is always perfect.

He loves us, he cares for us and His plan for us is peace (Yes, I will continue to repeat this because I want it to become implanted into our memory).

So let us cast our cares upon Him. Peace works better that way and we can't carry it anyway, we'll just stress ourselves out trying. Trust His timing because when He exalts us, it'll always be for His glory and not about us anyway.

I know it gets exciting and we just want to go after everything head first and that's great, but let us make sure we are waiting for God's timing and not working in our own strength. It may seem good now, but when the rubber meets the road, we'll find ourselves in a mess if we didn't wait for God.

Rest in that peace today, know that God cares for us and that we can truly cast our cares on Him and leave them there knowing that they will not be forgotten nor rejected, but responded to at exactly the right time.

Let us pray:

Father, today we just thank You for loving us and caring for us. We thank You for being a safe place where we can cast our cares and know that they are heard and never disregarded. We thank You for the zeal that you have placed in us to desire to do Your will and to go and follow hard after You. Father, we ask that You help us to use that zeal properly and that we not become so overzealous that we forget to consult You in our endeavors. Father, we thank You for being the protector of our peace and for just being the God of our peace. You are Jehovah Shalom and we know that Your plan for us is peace. Father, we ask that You help us to continue to walk in that peace daily and to continue to trust You in all of our ways so that we do not find ourselves stressed with trying to manage things on our own. Thank You for being trustworthy and thank You for showing us that we can indeed trust You at Your Word and at Your character. We humble ourselves before You and we wait for You to exalt us at the proper time. Father, help us to be patient in our waiting and not to stress while waiting. We make our daily confession that no matter what we face today, we will trust in You and we will not be afraid. We know that You know best and help us to stay reminded of that at times when we may get discouraged. We ask these things in the name of Christ Jesus, Amen.

Day 8
What do I need?
Philippians 4:19

We have spent some time in Philippians over the last few days. This chapter just gives us so much as it pertains to maintaining our peace. So today we journey down to the end of the chapter, "And my God shall supply all your need according to His riches in glory by Christ Jesus."

So what does this have to do with our faith? Well, I'm so glad you asked.

We all have needs right? Do we ever feel like those needs are not being met, or are in danger of not being met?

I think most of us can say we have been there before. We have worried about a bill getting paid, groceries being purchased or being able to get gas in the car.

This verse contains a simple reminder, God will supply. He has all that we need, He owns everything we have need of in this world and in heaven. He will supply.

Now this verse does not speak about those things that we just want (there are other verses that address that and we'll talk about that another day), but today we are talking about the things that we actually need.

We need clothes on our back, food to eat, water and lights in the house. This is our reassurance that He will supply.

It can become hard to maintain our peace when we are afraid that one of our basic needs will not be met.

Thanks be to God that we can take Him at His Word. Thanks be to God that we can trust that He will indeed supply our needs.

We can rest in that and we can take that to the bank. He will not let us fall and He will keep us in perfect peace as long as we remain focused on Him and seek Him first.

I cannot promise that we will never have trouble because trials are for our making, but I can promise that He will see us through and deliver us when the time is right. Everything is not meant for us to be released from immediately because often times there are things that we have to learn as we go through.

The question is will we trust Him and maintain our peace even while we are going through. That is how we determine if we are truly walking in peace. Not when things are going great, but when we find ourselves in need and we are waiting on God to come through. Will we kick and scream or will we rest in the peace that the Father brings?

We know that He will supply, His Word tells us just that, but we don't always know when it will happen. Can we maintain our peace in our waiting?

We can do it, I know we can. We can rest in His peace.

Let us pray:
Father today we first want to thank You for who You are. Thank You for being God in our lives. Thank You for being the author and the finisher of our faith and thank You for being Jehovah Jireh, our great provider. Father, we come to You recognizing that we have needs

and we will always have needs. No matter where we are in life, we will always have needs. We recognize that we do not meet these needs on our own, but it is in You that our needs are met. Father, today we just confess that we trust You to supply. We trust You to provide. We confess that no matter what we face today, we will trust in You and we will not be afraid. We trust You to be God in our lives. Father, we thank You for loving us and caring for us and desiring to see us walk in Your peace. Thank You for always knowing what is best for us. Thank You for sustaining our peace even in uncertain times. We rest in that peace Father and we carry it with us day by day. We make our daily confession that no matter what we face today, we will trust in You and we will not be afraid. Thank You for being a safe place where our hope can rest. We ask this, and all things, in the name of Christ Jesus, Amen.

Day 9
Still anxious?
Psalms 139:23-24

As I've been journeying through this devotional I have been reading a study plan in the Bible app entitled "Dangerous Prayers." Now I have read this plan before, but for some reason, this time it is hitting a little differently. Our scripture for today is one of the "dangerous prayers" that David prays, "Search me, O God, and know my heart; Try me, and know my anxieties; And see if there is any wicked way in me, And lead me in the way everlasting."

David calls out to God to search his heart, to try him and to know his anxieties. Then, not just that, he also asks God to see if there is any wicked in him and to lead him in the way everlasting. Now, if that isn't a dangerous prayer, I don't know what is.

Dangerous or not, if we want to experience peace, we too must be willing to pray this prayer. We cannot ask God to heal areas that we have not surrendered to Him. God is a perfect gentleman and He will not force himself upon us. If we don't invite Him in, we cannot expect Him to come in.

When we pray and ask God to search our hearts and to try us and know our anxieties, we are asking Him to stir up those things that threaten our peace. The initial response we see to this prayer may very well be a perceived increase of stress, but if we are going to pray this prayer, then we must be on guard and ready for

God to respond, because He most certainly will respond.

When we ask Him to try us, we are inviting Him to allow us to experience trials, these trials are what will reveal our anxieties. We must recognize them for what they are.

I will be the first to admit that when praying this prayer, I began to feel so overwhelmed like every little thing was getting on my nerves. What I came to realize was that I was sort of living life in this constant state of anxiety. I was walking around waiting for shoes to drop, so to speak, and not trusting God fully. I would have moments where I felt this sudden sense of dread and couldn't even identify what was causing it. Normally, what I would realize, is that it was something that I was worried about that I was trying to handle on my own instead of allowing God to handle it.

Guess what happened every time? Once I surrendered it to God, He handled it and showed me that He already had it worked out and I was just stressing myself out for nothing.

However, if we look a little further, David does not stop there, he continues on and asks God to see if there is any wicked way in him and to lead him in the way everlasting.

See, what happens is that when we fail to trust God, we find ourselves drifting into wickedness. It's not something that happens overnight, but we wake up one day and realize how far we have drifted because we dipped in a little bit of self here, a little bit of self there and a little bit of anxiousness here and next thing we know, we are so far gone and we don't even know how we got there. We've drifted so far in self because we kept trying to fix everything on our own instead of consulting God and now we are walking around with this overwhelming weight of anxiety over things that we were never even meant to carry.

When we find ourselves here though, there is good news. We are never so far that the Father can't reach us. We just have to ask Him to take control. We just have to invite Him into our situations and confess our wrong.

That is how we allow Him to lead us in the way everlasting. That is how we follow after Him. We surrender our will and pick up His will.

So today, let us pray this prayer together:

Father we come before You right now and we ask you to search our hearts oh God. We ask You to try us and to know our anxieties oh God. Not only that, but God we ask that as You try us, that You give us the strength and the wisdom to follow after You and to have eyes to see that which You reveal. Father, we ask that if there is any wicked way in us that You lead us in the way everlasting. Father, we confess our sin to You, those that we have done knowingly and unknowingly, we ask that You forgive us, cleanse us, purge us and help us to walk in the peace that You bring and not in the weight that we have picked up. Today we confess that no matter what we face today, we will trust in You and we will not be afraid. We surrender to You. We relinquish control so that You can be the driver in our lives. We recognize that we have tried it our way long enough and that has only lead us to stress and anxiety. That is not Your will for us and we recognize that Your will is what is best. Help us to walk in Your will, Your way and Your peace, in the name of Jesus we pray, Amen.

Day 10
So where is my peace?
Isaiah 26:3

Full transparency, I pick back up here after taking a
break for several days from writing because life had
become hectic and I honestly had begun to forget
about my writing, but this day, God told me to write so
here were are.

As, I continue to remind you, we are on this journey
together and with that comes transparency and reality.
Let's be honest, as we go through this journey we may
get off track and miss several days, but that's just fine.
Just come back. That's all I ask. Come back and re-
engage.

So today we journey to the book of Isaiah and in the
midst of the prophetic word he is delivering, we find a
word of peace, "You will keep him in perfect peace,
Whose mind is stayed on You, Because he trusts in
You."

Let's break this down.

If you're like me, you may find this to be a familiar
passage of scripture. I even have a song come to mind
with these words. God will keep us in perfect peace
when our minds are stayed on Him.

We sometimes miss that last piece of the verse though,
"because he trusts in you."

We get that first part down. Father keep me in perfect
peace, my mind is stayed on you. All the while He is
waiting for us to trust Him.

Trust is the key.

That is why we are kept in perfect peace when our minds are stayed on Him, it is because we trust Him. It is easy to continue to look to God and ask for peace while still looking for our own way to do things and not trusting Him, but we won't find peace that way. When we do it that way we are hovering over the doorstep with one foot in and one foot out. We're crying, "God I need your peace, but God I don't know if you're going to do this the way I need you to so let me keep my hands on it too."

Where is our peace in that?

NON-EXISTENT

We receive peace because of trust. We receive peace because we acknowledge that we are finite beings, but our infinite God knows best ALWAYS and we can rest in that.

Our peace is a result of our trust.

So as we are searching for peace along this journey, let us remember that it is our trust in God that rewards us peace because we have stopped trying to manage things on our own and have decided to turn things over to the God of the universe who created us and can manage our lives much much better than we ever could ourselves.

Let us pray:

Father, today we come to You and we recognize that we need peace. Father, we recognize that things may be getting rough around us and that we sometimes do not even know which way is up. Father, we acknowledge Your might and Your power and we admit that we are nothing without You. Father, today we ask that you come into our hearts and help us to trust You all the more. Father, we know that You are good, that You are gracious and that You are perfect, help us to receive Your perfect peace. Help us not to only keep our minds stayed on You, but to also trust You. We know that is where our peace lies and that is how we enter into Your rest. Thank You for loving us and keeping us. Father, we confess that no matter what we face today, we will trust in You and we will not be afraid. We surrender our will to yours and we enter into Your peace. Thank You for Your perfect peace oh God. We love You and we thank You in the name of Jesus, Amen.

Day 11
It's already done?
Isaiah 53:5

We don't always know what to do or how to think. We don't always know how to respond when that feeling of overwhelming dread comes upon us. We may not even know how to move forward when we get stuck in that place of stress, but God has covered us.

Our verse today reminds us that everything we need, as it pertains to peace, was already accomplished on calvary. "But He was wounded for our transgressions, He was bruised for our iniquities; The chastisement for our peace was upon Him, And by His stripes we are healed."

He did it and it's done. He was wounded for our transgressions. He was wounded for the wrong we would do. He was wounded so that we would not have to pay the ultimate price. He was bruised for our iniquities. He was bruised for our uncleanliness so that we could be cleaned. He took the punishment so that we could be forgiven and cleansed.

And then, here it is, the chastisement for our peace was upon Him. He took the chastisement so that we could have peace. He took the punishment so that we could have peace.

Do we dare to walk into that peace?

He already did it. He already took the punishment, we don't have to keep punishing ourselves because He took it all. He took the wounding, he took the bruising, he took the chastisement. He did it so we didn't have to.

We have only to walk in that peace.

We can walk in peace knowing that our sin is covered.

We can walk in peace knowing that our iniquities are purged.

We can walk in peace knowing that He paid the ultimate price so we don't have to.

He did it, it's done. Period.

AND by His stripes, we are healed.

We ARE healed.

Not that we will be healed, not that we were healed, but we ARE healed.

Not just physical healing, but mental and emotional healing as well. That is where our peace lies.

We claim that nothing that comes against us shall be able to take away our peace, because our minds are healed.

No longer will we torment ourselves with thoughts of pain and anxiety, we will receive the perfect healing that the Savior bore for us.

We receive the peace that He suffered for.

Today we speak peace over ourselves. No matter what comes against us, we will trust in Him and we will not be afraid.

It's already done.

Let us pray:
Father, we thank You for being You. We thank You for Your perfect peace and Your perfect protection over us. Thank You for every sacrifice You made for us. Thank

You for bearing our punishment. Thank You for the gift of peace. We receive that gift. We do not reject it. We welcome Your peace to come into our lives and to flow into every hidden place that tries to threaten our peace. We admit that we need You in every aspect of our lives and that we are nothing apart from You. Thank You Father for keeping us. Thank You Father for protecting us. Thank You for bearing the punishment and providing us peace. We honor You today by openly accepting what You have provided. We ask that You help us to receive this gift daily. We ask that even when we become discouraged and we want to give up, that You will help us to admit and declare that we are Yours and that we have peace. We proclaim peace over every negative thought that tries to tell us that there is not peace. We tear down every stronghold that attempts to exalt itself against the knowledge of You. We give those strongholds no power and we run to You our strong tower and the protector of our peace. We give You glory honor and praise and we thank You for victory. In the name of Jesus, Amen!

Day 12
Where's my help?
Psalms 121:1-3

Sometimes we just need help. We get frustrated, we get confused, we get overwhelmed and we need help.
So where do we look? "I will lift up my eyes to the hills— From whence comes my help? My help comes from the LORD, Who made heaven and earth. He will not allow your foot to be moved; He who keeps you will not slumber."
To the hills is where we can look. That is where our help comes from, the God of heaven and earth.
When we don't know where to look, we can look up to the Father.
What happens when we look up? The first thing is that it takes our focus off of our situation and places it on the Father who is in control of it all. That is why we can say that is where our help comes from, because He is in control.
Oh what peace, to focus on a loving Father instead of turmoil around us.
When we seem to be drowning under the expectations of others, we can look up.
When we feel that we cannot do anything right, we can look up.
When we feel that pain is so much more prevalent than peace, we can look up.
He sees us, He knows us and He will not allow our foot to be moved. He does not slumber, He does not

sleep, He is always aware of our every hurt, our every pain, our every need. He is our help.

Looking within can bring us so much more pain and anxiety because we know that we cannot handle it on our own, but looking up transfers the expectation from within to our faithful and loving Father.

Even if we can't handle it, He can.

"He who keeps you will not slumber." The keeper of our souls does not slumber. He never grows tired of looking after us. We never have to worry that we are not kept because we are forever and always kept by Him.

That should bring us so much peace, to know that the one who keeps us is forever watching. He does not take a break, he does not leave us hanging, but He keeps us.

That is why we can stand knowing that we can look to Him, because He is always there.

So when we ask where is our help, the answer is undoubtedly found in the Father.

Let us pray:
Father, thank You. Thank You for being our help. Thank You that we can look to You knowing that You are where our help comes from. Thank You that You continually keep us and You do not grow tired of keeping us. We admit that we hurt sometimes and that we stumble sometimes. We admit that sometimes we get overwhelmed and we can forget where to look, but Father today we ask that You help us to remember to look to You. We make our daily confession that no

matter what we face today, we will trust in You and we will not be afraid. We know that with that trust, it involves us looking to You for our help and not to ourselves. Father, we commit ourselves and our peace to You, knowing that You are the only One who can keep them both. Thank You for keeping us. Go with us today Father, we invite You in. Lead us in Your peace and Your righteousness and help us not to be overwhelmed. We surrender all to You, in the name of Jesus we pray, Amen.

Day 13
Rest, how?
Matthew 11:28-30

Life gets hard at times. We get overwhelmed and we sometimes do not know what to do next, but we can take courage in the fact that He will give us rest.

"Come to Me, all you who labor and are heavy laden, and I will give you rest. Take My yoke upon you and learn from Me, for I am gentle and lowly in heart, and you will find rest for your souls. For My yoke is easy and My burden is light."

We weren't made to carry these burdens alone. We weren't made to struggle alone and we definitely were not made to bury our cares and keep going on as if nothing is wrong.

So what do we do when we feel overwhelmed and we do not know how to carry it all?

The answer lies here in the scriptures. We go to the Father. The one who made us and created us and cares for us. We go to Him and allow Him to give us rest. We take His yoke upon us and learn from Him. His yoke is easy and His burden is light.

For those who do not know what a yoke is, a yoke is a wooden beam used by a pair of oxen so that they can carry a load together.

When we take the Father's yoke upon us, we allow Him to carry the burden with us and I don't know any better person to be yoked up with than the Father.

He is stronger than us, and His burden is light.

Imagine going to the Father carrying a heavy load, connecting to His yoke, placing the load on that yoke and allowing Him to carry it with us! My God! What an image, surely we will find rest there.

Then, we go to the scripture and He tells us that His yoke is easy and His burden is light. His yoke is easy because He can carry the load so much better than we can. His burden is light because He does not add any weight to our load to carry. He takes what we are carrying and helps us through.

But here's the catch...

We have to come to Him. We cannot just sit around looking for Him to come and get us if we have not invited Him into our situations.

Oh but when we come to Him, we will find rest for our souls.

Oh what peace! Finding rest at the Father's side.

Let us pray:
Father, today we thank You for peace. We thank You for being a place we can go to and find rest. Right now Father, we come to You. We admit and we recognize that we need Your help. We admit that we cannot carry these burdens alone and we need You to come in and help us. We invite You into our situations. We invite You to come in and be God and help us. Carry this burden with us Father. We take up Your yoke and we rest our burdens on You. As we lay them down, we find rest and God, we receive Your rest. Thank You for being a place of rest for us. Thank You for caring for us so deeply and compassionately. Thank You for

carrying our load. We give You glory oh God and we honor You just for who You are. As we daily confess, no matter what we face today, we will trust in You and we will not be afraid...because we know that You are with us and there is no burden that we must carry alone. Thank You for that. We commit ourselves and this day into Your hands, have Your way in us. In the matchless name of Jesus we pray, Amen!

Day 14
Leaning where?
Proverbs 3:5-6

It isn't always easy to trust in the Lord. I can admit
that, but can we agree that it should be? When we look
to His track record and all that He has done then and
now, it should be easy for us to trust Him, right?
Proverbs tells us, "Trust in the LORD with all your
heart, And lean not on your own understanding; In all
your ways acknowledge Him, And He shall direct your
paths."
So, what is it that makes it hard? We could probably
agree that it is often when we lean to our own
understanding that makes it hard to trust in Him.
We see things in terms of our own finite thinking and it
can cause us to forget that God is bigger than any
situation we face. It can distract us from remembering
all the times that He has proven Himself, but when we
find ourselves leaning to our own understanding, our
own finite thinking, that should be our nudge to lean
into the Father and His complete vision and wisdom.
We cannot always see the big picture, but God can.
When we acknowledge Him in all of our ways, we
allow Him to direct our paths as opposed to us trying
to direct our own paths.
Trying to direct our own paths can be a huge threat to
our peace. We can never see all that is up ahead. When
we think we have it all figured out and try to lead
ourselves, we find ourselves in a mess.

On the other hand, when we acknowledge the Father and trust in His leading and His guidance, we allow Him to direct our paths and that brings us peace.

He won't force His direction upon us. When we acknowledge Him in all our ways, we invite His direction in our lives.

Each decision we make, when we ask Him to lead us, He will.

That is how we trust Him, every step of the way. We make it a point to seek His direction in every move we make, from the big things to the little things. He cares about them all and He will direct us in them all.

We find our peace in trusting in Him and taking the pressure off of ourselves. We can't do it within ourselves anyway, so why not just trust in the One who created us and stop stressing ourselves out?

Let us pray:
Father, today we just say thank You. We thank You for Your peace and for Your perfect leading in our lives. We submit our will to Yours and we invite You to guide us. Father, we acknowledge that we don't know everything and that we need Your direction. Today we ask that You direct our paths. We acknowledge You and we put our trust in You. We make our daily confession that no matter what we face today, we will trust in You and we will not be afraid. We trust You because we know Who You are. We know Your track record and we know that although we don't see the big picture, You do. Father, have Your way in us today. Lead us into Your perfect peace, direct our paths and order our

steps. We need You. We thank You in advance, this we pray in the name of Jesus, Amen.

Day 15
What comfort?
Psalms 94:19

Sometimes we just need to be comforted. We go through many trials in life and our feelings are very real and valid. When we don't know where to place our frustrations and anxieties, we can always lay them at the feet of the Father.

This Psalm addresses this very concern, "In the multitude of my anxieties within me, Your comforts delight my soul."

It is perfectly fine for us to be honest with God about how we feel. In all actuality, He is the only one who can exchange our anxieties for comfort.

When anxiety comes to threaten our peace, we can lay it at His feet and receive His comfort in exchange.

We can be honest and admit that we can experience a multitude of anxieties at times. Life gets hard, the kids are acting crazy, the spouse doesn't get it, my friends are all preoccupied with their hectic lives and we just don't know which way is up. We try to talk to our spouse, but they don't even know how to comprehend what we're facing. We try to talk to our friends, but they are going through and we end up being their listening ear instead and then all the while, we are trying to manage work, marriage, parenting and ministry.

Anxieties pile on and our peace is in serious danger. But God.

His Word says that when this is how I feel at my very core, His comfort will be there to delight my soul. But we might be wondering, how do we go from anxiety to comfort?

I am no Bible scholar, but as I learn more and more about the Father and His character, I can only believe that we must do the work.

We must go to Him and lay our concerns at His feet. We can be raw and honest with Him about how we feel, I promise He can handle it.

As we lay our concerns at His feet, we exchange our anxieties, for His comfort, His peace.

When we go to Him, we are spending time with Him. We are coming to Him and inviting Him into our situations. We are saying, "God I can't do this without You." As we invite Him in, He responds by sending His comfort to delight our souls.

His comfort does not erase any of what is going on in our lives, but it helps us to change our perspective. We can see it differently and carry it lighter because we have changed our viewpoint from focusing on our anxieties, to focusing on the Author and Finisher of our lives. Therein lies our peace, in the One whose comfort delights our souls. Will you invite Him in today?

Let us pray:
Father today we come to You recognizing that we need You. You are so loving, so caring, so compassionate and kind and we thank You for being all that You are in our lives. We admit that things are seemingly crazy, we

are getting overwhelmed and anxiety is coming in and threatening our peace, but Father we know that You are greater than it all. Father we surrender it all to You. We lay it all at You feet because we know that You can handle it. Thank You for carrying our burdens and providing us such comfort that is a delight to our souls. We daily confess to You that no matter what we face today, we will trust in You and we will not be afraid. With that confession, we surrender our anxieties to You. We give You our children, we give You our relationships, we give You our jobs and we allow You to show us how to manage them all when we do not know what to do next. Help us to be good spouses, good parents, good friends, good employees and to do all of these things to Your glory. We receive Your comfort that delights our souls. We rest in your loving arms and allow You to care for us. Thank You for just being God. We are nothing without You and we know that we need You in everything that we do. Have Your way in us today and everyday. We are Yours. We pray this in Jesus's name, Amen.

Day 16
Rest, again?
Matthew 11:28-30

I know you may be saying, we just did these verses a
few days ago and you are correct, we did. The Spirit of
the Lord is leading me to revisit them though. I
received some new teaching in regard to these verses
and, while I thought of rewriting Day 13, I know that
devotion was God breathed for that particular day and
so here we are again on Day 16 with rest once again.
To refresh our memories, the verses read, "Come to
Me, all you who labor and are heavy laden, and I will
give you rest. Take My yoke upon you and learn from
Me, for I am gentle and lowly in heart, and you will
find rest for your souls. For My yoke is easy and My
burden is light."
Upon further teaching and revelation, I have learned
that the truest translation of "yoke" in this scripture is
considered the Rabbi's teaching. In the middle eastern
context, when someone wanted to learn or interpret
something of scripture, they would go to the Rabbi and
ask him to share his yoke with them. The yoke was the
Rabbi's interpretation of scripture.
So when we take this scripture in that context, it gives
it a whole new light, but still such a true revelation of
peace.
The Father is calling us to take His teaching, His
interpretation of scripture upon us and learn of him.
Wow! Still, what peace that brings!

We often find ourselves interpreting scripture in ways that God has not intended and we do indeed begin to feel burdened and heavy laden. We find ourselves trying to keep up with a list of commands, as opposed to understanding God's heart in the scriptures.

I journeyed through *Jesus and Women* by Kristi McLelland[1] and if I did not learn anything else, I learned how to view scripture and ask myself what does it teach me about God as opposed to asking what does it teach me about myself.

When we take the Father's yoke upon us, we learn His heart in the scriptures. We see His character and we understand that goodness is His nature. That in itself should bring us peace.

He then reminds us that He is gentle and lowly of heart and that we will find rest for our souls.

He is gentle and lowly of heart. His desire is not for us to feel burdened or that relationship with Him is keeping a list of do's and don'ts. He wants us to know that He is a gentle and loving Father. When He chastises us, it is with grace and when He teaches us, it is gently.

His yoke is easy and His burden is light. When we feel burdened and heavy laden, these are burdens that we have placed upon ourselves, but the Father is inviting us to come to Him, to bring our burdens and our cares to Him, to lay them at His feet and allow Him, the gentle, loving Father, to bring us rest.

There is indeed rest for our souls.

Let us pray:

Father, today we come to You with new knowledge. We come to You with increased fervor and a greater desire to understand your teachings. Father, we want to hear from You and we want to learn of You. Father, we come asking You to give us Your yoke. We have tried to understand on our own, we have brought ourselves undue burdens, but we surrender that to You now. We confess, God, that we want to receive Your rest. We receive what You bring and we lay aside every weight that desires to hinder us. Thank You for being a gentle and loving Father. Thank You for keeping us. We make our daily confession that Father, no matter what we face today, we will trust in You and we will not be afraid. We are open and ready to receive from You. Come into our lives, come into our homes, come into our jobs and have Your mighty way in us. We are here for You oh God. In the name of Jesus we pray, Amen.

Day 17
What Can I Do?
Hebrews 12:14

A pastor that I know and love said something so profound regarding this scripture and I just had to share it with you, my amazing readers. "Peace does not just come to us, we must go after it."

Today's scripture reads, "Pursue peace with all people, and holiness, without which no one will see the Lord:" As we have been walking through this journey to peace, it has become so apparent that we have to do some work if we are going to find peace. We must pursue it with all people. We must recognize what we can control and what we cannot control. That which we can control, we make adjustments to and that which we cannot control, we lay it down and keep it moving.

We cannot control people. The sooner we reach that realization, the sooner we will become free.

There are many things that come at us that we have no control over, but we must be willing to take charge of that which we can control under the leading of Holy Spirit.

We find ourselves faced with so many daily challenges that attempt to threaten our peace, but each day, we have a choice to pursue peace.

When we get that bad doctor's report, pursue peace. When we get that unexpected bill, pursue peace. When we hear that a friend was speaking negatively about us behind our back, pursue peace. When we get into that argument with our significant other, pursue peace. When the kids just won't seem to act right, pursue peace.

We have the option and the ability to pursue peace. Pursuing peace doesn't mean that we ignore our situations or that we just walk away from them without a second thought. Pursuing peace may even often mean that we address these situations head on and identify exactly what we need.

Pursuing peace may involve us going to the feet of the Father to seek direction for how to proceed in each situation.

These are very real issues that we face and no one can expect us to just move on past them like they do not exist, but we do not let them take us out. We do not just sit idly by and allow them to consume us and we do not sit idly and say, "peace is coming," we MUST do our part.

We make a daily choice to pursue peace because we know the One who created us and Who holds our lives in His hands.

We take that doctor's report and lay it at the feet of Jesus because though we can't carry it, He can.

We take that unexpected bill and present it to the Father because He is the author and finisher of our faith and all that we have need of He has already provided.

We confront that friend in love (as Holy Spirit leads) to get the real story and not just respond based on hearsay.

We resolve issues with our significant other in love so that we do not allow the root of bitterness to spring up. We discipline our children in the best way we know and we present them to the Father and ask Him to touch their hearts, minds and behavior to line up to be just who He has created them to be.

We don't sit still and expect peace to just come, but we pursue it, daily. This is what we can do. Though we cannot control others, we can control our response. When we actively respond in pursuit of peace, peace has no choice but to be found by us.

Let us pray:
Father, we thank You for reminding us to pursue peace with all people. Father, we thank You for reminding us of what we can do and the active role we play in our pursuit of peace. Father, we honor You for being the Great I Am and we recognize that it is You who provides us peace. We confess that no matter we face today, we will trust in You and we will not be afraid. No matter what may come against us today, we surrender it to You and we allow You to have free reign in our lives. Father, we make a conscious decision to pursue peace. We submit our will to Yours and we ask that You come in and lead and guide our every step. Show us how to pursue peace in each situation so that we do not find ourselves kicking against the goads. Father, in all things we want to be in Your will and we know that Your will and Your plan for us is peace. Have Your way in us, use us for Your glory and

continue to bestow upon us Your peace. We thank You and we praise You in the name of Jesus, Amen!

Day 18
Above ALL?
Ephesians 3:20

Whatever we're thinking, or imagining, He can do more.

We can have issues and situations in our lives that seem impossible. We have worked out in our minds the way that we are expecting things to work out and how we expect God to move. Can I help you for a moment? Whatever we're thinking…He can do more!

Ephesians tells us, "Now to Him who is able to do exceedingly abundantly above all that we ask or think, according to the power that works in us,"

Often times we disrupt our own peace by thinking that we have already worked though every possible outcome and that we know exactly what's going to happen. We think that there is no way that a situation can work out in our favor and we stress ourselves out with our perceived outcomes.

Allow me to bring your attention back to our scripture for the day. He can do exceedingly abundantly above ALL that we can ask or think. That means that those situations we think we have already worked out in our heads, He can work them out better.

The outcomes to which we think we have already evaluated all alternatives, He can do more. He can do exceedingly abundantly more.

When we look at the phrase "exceedingly abundantly," we can break it down to see just how much our Father is able to do.

First, we define abundantly. Abundantly means excessive, overflowing or surplus, just to name a few. We then add exceedingly, which means to an extreme degree.

When we put the two together, we see that, to an extreme degree, God is able to do excessively, overflowing and in surplus more that we can ask or think.

Oh what peace! To know that our finite minds cannot comprehend all that our Father can do and whatever we're thinking it is, well, He's going way beyond ALL of that.

That takes the pressure off of us and allows us to just trust in what the Father can do. But let's not leave out the end of the verse, "according to the power that works in us."

Just as we discussed yesterday, we can't sit idly by and expect peace to find us. The power is at work within us. God has placed the power and authority within us. We ask and we think and then we allow God to be God. We pursue peace by trusting the power that is at work within us. We don't stress ourselves by overthinking or even believing that we have to work it out on our own. We simply open our mouths and present our needs to the Father and trust Him to work it out, through us, as only He can. Above ALL we can ask or think is what He is able to do. That is what we should believe Him to do as we rest in the peace in knowing that He is in control of every situation.

Let us pray:

Father, we thank You for being God in our lives. We thank You for being the perfecter and keeper of our peace. Father, today we ask that You would come into our every situation and rule in such a way that only You can. Today we confess that no matter what we face, we will trust in You and we will not be afraid. We will not fear unknown outcomes and we will not fear outcomes that we have manufactured in our minds. We know that You can do more than anything we can ask or think. We know that You have the final say and that You can work out every situation better than we could ever imagine. We surrender our will to Yours and we allow You to have your way in every situation. We avail ourselves that Your power may be made manifest within us and that Your will be done through us. All these things we ask in the precious name of Jesus, Amen!

Day 19
So…Keep Heart?
Galatians 6:9

Have you ever found yourself trying to figure out
when is my break coming?

We feel we have been through so much and so much
seems to be coming against us that we can see no end
in sight. What a place of distress that can put us in.
That can definitely threaten our peace.

When it seems that we cannot catch a break, it can be
hard to keep heart.

Galatians provides us with this gentle reminder
though, "And let us not grow weary while doing good,
for in due season we shall reap if we do not lose
heart."

Don't lose heart. It may seem rough and it may at
times seem like we should give up, but don't lose
heart. There's still more, better is ahead and God is still
working on our behalf.

In due season, we shall reap.

I'll be the first to admit that waiting for that due season
can be challenging. We don't know when that due
season will be, but what we do know is that God's
timing is perfect.

I can only believe that due season is God's appointed
time. We may not know when due season is coming,
but we do know Who determines when it comes.

This gives us good reason to keep heart.

We can keep heart because we can trust that the Father who loves us has already predestined our due season and His plans and thoughts for us are good.

We can keep heart because we know that our time is coming. It may not be today, tomorrow, or even a week from now, but we can take each struggle as an opportunity to learn and to grow.

This should offer us peace as we journey through our daily trials. Nothing that we face is intended to destroy us, but only to build us. We can make it through if we keep our focus on the Father.

So I encourage you today, don't lose heart, hang in there, God has great things planned for us in due season, we need only to keep heart.

Let us pray:

Father, we come to You today asking that You help us to keep heart. We know that it is so much easier said than done and it is a challenge daily to keep heart in the midst of the struggle. Father, knowing this, we also know that with You, we can keep heart. We know that with You, we can make it. We trust You for the bringing about of our due season and we wait with expectancy for the harvest that is coming. Thank You for being more than enough for us and for always having the best plans for us. We stand on our daily confession that no matter what we face, we will trust in You and we will not be afraid. We thank You for being the lover and keeper of our souls and for always working things out better than we imagine. We stand on Your Word today and we confess that we will keep heart because

You are in control. All these things we ask in the name of Jesus, Amen.

Day 20
I'm Blessed?
Numbers 6:24-26

"The LORD bless you and keep you; The LORD make His face shine upon you, And be gracious to you; The LORD lift up His countenance upon you, And give you peace."

We start today with this blessing the Lord instructed Moses to have Aaron to deliver to the children of Israel in the book of Numbers. While this blessing was given to the children of Israel, I believe it still extends to us today.

When we feel discouraged and we feel that threat to our peace, we can be encouraged knowing that the favor and blessings of the Father are upon us.

He will bless us and keep us daily. Whenever we feel low and we feel that anxiety trying to set in, we need only to remember that He is with us. His face is shining upon us and He is oh so gracious to us.

When we don't want to be kept or even know that we need to be kept, He keeps us.

What an assurance of peace to know that we are children of a Father who is keeping us even when we are unaware of what we need.

His graciousness is more than we could ever imagine or hope for. Goodness is His very nature. He extends to us grace that we do not deserve and He gives us grace to handle life's circumstances daily. It is His grace that keeps us.

I wake up each day and ask God to give me the grace to handle whatever I face that day. I encourage you to do the same. We need His grace, we would be no where and nothing without it.

He lifts His countenance upon us and He gives us peace.

When we find ourselves in stressful situations, just to know that His countenance is upon us should bring us peace.

When we find ourselves feeling overwhelmed and we cannot see what is coming next, just think on this thought, *"He sees me."*

That right there brings me such peace. To know that He sees me. To lift his countenance upon us is to see us. I hope that it also brings you peace. When we know that He sees us and we know that He is gracious to us, we know that He is faithful to act on our behalf at the appointed time. Even when he appears to be silent or still, we can trust His graciousness toward us to intervene when the time is right. We need not to fret or to worry, we can rest in the knowledge that He is concerned with our every concern and His desire is to bring us peace.

Whatever it is, whatever we're going through, however impossible it seems, just know He sees us. His countenance is lifted upon us and His face is shining upon us. He, the lover of our souls and the keeper of our hearts is bringing us peace.

Let us pray:

Father, today we thank You for bringing us peace. We thank You for being so gracious to us and for making your face to shine upon us. We are grateful that Your countenance is lifted upon us and we rest in the peace that You bring. Father, today we pray and ask that You continue to extend Your grace to us to handle all that we face today and everyday. We confess that no matter what we face today, we will trust in You and we will not be afraid. We recognize that we can do nothing without You, but with You, we can do all things. Have Your way in us today, we surrender to Your will for us and we ask that You continue to bless us and keep us each and every day. We rest in the peace of knowing that You indeed do keep us and we are grateful for Your all sufficient knowledge that protects us even in our ignorance. We love You and we praise You and we know that all that we are is because of You. All these things we pray in the name of Your son Jesus, amen!

Day 21
Soo…I win?
Exodus 14:14

Here we are at the end of our journey, we have made it to day 21. It is my prayer that, through this journey, you have been able to access the peace that God promises us in the scriptures.

Today we end here knowing that in the end, we win. Exodus 14:14 tells us that, "The LORD will fight for you, and you shall hold your peace."

It's a fixed fight. We have already won, we need only to allow the Lord to fight for us. As he fights, we need only to hold our peace, to be still.

The Lord has given us peace. He has provided for us the way to victory. We don't have to fight for ourselves because the Lord has it under control.

When finances aren't lining up, we can hold our peace, the Lord is fighting for us.

When things at home are going crazy, we can hold our peace, the Lord is fighting for us.

When work is becoming overly stressful, we can hold our peace, the Lord is fighting for us.

When the children are constantly getting into trouble, we can hold our peace, the Lord is fighting for us.

Each and every day and each and every way, as we journey through life, we never know what is to come, but we can always remember to hold our peace because the Lord is fighting for us.

We can stand on our daily confession, *"God no matter what I face today, I will trust in You and I will not be afraid."*

We can stand on this because we know that the Lord is fighting for us. In all things, through all things, He is fighting for us, He will always fight for us and we shall hold our peace.

We shall indeed hold our peace. The peace that we have tapped into, that we have committed to hold onto as we have journeyed through these days, we shall continue to hold onto that peace. We will not reject it and it will not be robbed from us, we shall hold onto it. This is our declaration,

"The peace that Christ died for on calvary is mine, I receive it, I walk in it and I confess that I will not allow it to be stolen from me nor will I willingly surrender it. I will hold onto it at all costs for I know that peace is God's plan for me."

As we stated at the beginning, He is our Jehovah Shalom, God of Peace. He will always be peace for us, in us and to us. He is peace in all things because He will fight for us in all things. We can rest in His promise and we can rest in His peace.

Let us pray:
Father, we thank You for fighting for us. We thank You for being our peace in every circumstance. Thank You for going with us through this journey. Thank You for reminding us of Your perfect peace. We stand in Your peace and we stand on Your peace. We openly receive Your peace daily. We know that apart from You there is

no peace and we make a conscious decision to walk with You daily. Thank You for just being You in our lives. Thank You for caring enough for us to continuously extend Your grace to us each day. We know that we don't deserve it and we could never repay You, but still You love us and continue to keep us each day. As we continue on our journey, even now, we ask that You help us to hold on to our peace and to remember and revisit every lesson that we have learned on this journey. We surrender all to You, knowing that as we take our hands off of it, we allow ourselves to rest in Your peace because we know You are in control. Thank You for being God and thank You for loving us so perfectly. All these things we ask in the precious name of Jesus, Amen!

Conclusion

We are not perfect beings and the reality is that we may stray at times. Life can overwhelm us and we can get distracted so I encourage you to return to this as often as you need to and refocus on the Source of your peace to give you strength for the journey ahead.
"These things I have spoken to you, that in Me you may have peace. In the world you will have tribulation; but be of good cheer, I have overcome the world." John 16:33
Tribulation will come, that is a guarantee; however, our Father God has already overcome it all and that is an even greater guarantee. I am thankful for the Father who has overcome the world. Let us go forth and take heart knowing that whatever we face, He has already overcome. With God, we can! I'm praying for each of you!

Notes

1. McLelland, Kristi. Jesus and Women-Bible Study Book: In the First Century and Now. Lifeway Press. 2020.

Acknowledgements

I must first give honor to God for gracing me and gifting me with the words to write. I've been journeying through this devotional over and over as I have prepared to release it to the world and each time I have been in awe of all the Father has spoken through me.

I must admit that I fully expected to have this to you all well before now, but as they say, life be life-ing and I found myself repeatedly pushing back the release date for one reason or another. Nonetheless, we serve and on time God and His timing is perfect so I trust that the release is right on time for the very souls He desires to reach.

I must thank my sister and my friend Zainab Mustapha for this amazing cover design. She worked a miracle because I really gave her no direction, just full creative license and I LOVE what she came up with.

I also must thank my brother Kelvin Holtzclaw for doing my photoshoot for the lovely photo that you see pictured on the back cover.

Big thanks to Bishop Jerome Rogers who provided me with invaluable teaching and instruction during my time serving at Strait Gate Deliverance Center.

I am thankful for my family and friends who have supported, encouraged and even nudged me along the way with the reminder to stop procrastinating.

Lastly, but certainly not least, I am thankful for all of my readers. I really pray that this will bless you just as much as it has blessed me along the way, if not more. Peace is so vital for our lives and I hope that this is daily encouragement for you to truly pursue peace for all your days, even on the hard days, especially on the hard days.

Be blessed, I love you and I promise you I mean it.

www.ingramcontent.com/pod-product-compliance
Lightning Source LLC
Chambersburg PA
CBHW031149090426
42738CB00008B/1276